Bird on Vacation
Jackie Tidey

Contents

My Bird Book	2
In Our Yard	4
At the Beach	6
At the Lake	8
In the Street	10
At the Bird Park	12
Glossary	16

My Bird Book

I have made a bird book.

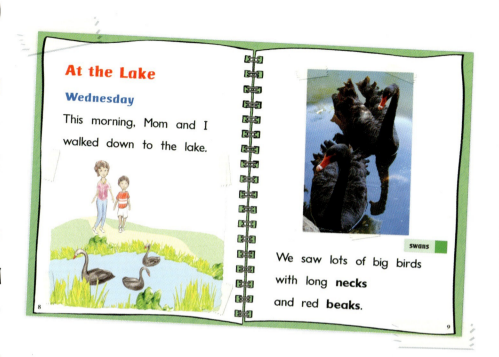

My book has words
and pictures of the birds
I saw this week.

In Our Yard

Monday

Today, I saw two birds in our yard.

doves

They had gray feathers. Some of the feathers had little white spots.

At the Beach

Tuesday

Mom and I had a picnic at the beach today.

Some birds ran up to us.

seagulls

They wanted some food.

We did not let them have our food,
so they flew away.

At the Lake

Wednesday

This morning, Mom and I walked down to the lake.

swans

We saw lots of big birds with long **necks** and red **beaks**.

In the Street

Thursday

Mom and I saw
lots of birds in a tree.

They had green and blue
and red feathers.

The birds liked the seeds in the trees.

At the Bird Park

Friday

Dad came to the bird park with us today.

We went into a **bird blind** at the park.

The bird blind had windows for us to look out at the birds.

A white bird with long legs flew over the water by us.

I saw lots of birds this week.

I like to look at birds and draw them, too.

Glossary

beaks

bird blind

necks